1

No diving

No running

2

No diving

No running

This collection of short wordless picture books helps to support children with speech, language and communication needs as they develop their expressive sentence and narrative skills through storytelling. Each book is comprised of six colourful images that follow a simple everyday routine such as 'Brushing Teeth', 'Having a Haircut' and 'Walking the Dog'. Unlike traditional picture books, they follow a film scroll effect, showing the progression of time and allowing the child to follow the story to its resolution. Because of their simplicity, the books can support children as they move from simple to intermediate sentence levels, as well as encouraging them to consider additional elements of language such as cause and effect, sequencing and inference.

This resource includes:

• Ten beautifully illustrated picture books, each following a simple pattern of routine, disruption and resolution

• An accompanying guidebook including story scripts, cue questions and prompts for using the resource to support additional skills

Although developed specifically to help children with speech, language and communication needs, this set is suitable for any child who requires support and practice in developing their speech. It is an invaluable resource for speech and language therapists, teaching staff and caregivers.

Kulvinder Kaur has received training in Applied Behavioural Analysis and has taught children between the ages of 2 and 16 years for 15 years. Her work has been mainly 1:1 with both verbal and non-verbal children. The Applied Behavioural Analysis curriculum covers mainly language, communication, social, cognitive, functional and academic skills. She currently works as a Team Lead on programmes, involving assessing skills, designing targets, creating lesson plans as well as producing resources. Alongside her role, Kulvinder continues to develop her practical teaching skills by educating children with a diagnosis of autism in mainstream primary schools and in private practice, which has involved working with behavioural analysts, speech and language therapists and multidisciplinary teams. She is the author of *Wordless Picture Books and Guide*, published by Speechmark in April 2016.

A **Speechmark** Book

Routledge
Taylor & Francis Group
www.routledge.com

EDUCATION

ISBN 978-0-367-34045-2

9 780367 340452

Routledge titles are available as eBook editions in a range of digital formats

an informa business